IGNITE YOUR INNER GENIE

BOOK 1

Rebecca Whitehall

BALBOA
PRESS

A DIVISION OF HAY HOUSE

Balboa Press books may be ordered through booksellers or by contacting:

Balboa Press
A Division of Hay House
1663 Liberty Drive
Bloomington, IN 47403
www.balboapress.com
1 (877) 407-4847

ISBN: 978-1-5043-7244-2 (sc)
ISBN: 978-1-5043-7245-9 (e)

Library of Congress Control Number: 2016921460

Print information available on the last page.

Balboa Press rev. date: 01/27/2017

Aladdin's Treasure

lamp genie

treasure

ring genie

merchant

wish

jewels

lamp

coins

brain

create

focus

job

listen

don't listen

brain

create

negative

positive

Word Search

```
B  E  Y  S  A  M  M  A  T  C  S  X  S  H  O
R  Z  Y  L  Z  P  P  T  O  B  I  T  H  O  C
A  B  G  O  Z  A  S  I  D  P  H  U  S  S  X
I  Y  O  H  S  D  N  H  M  I  Y  G  I  P  W
N  Q  E  A  I  S  J  E  W  E  L  S  W  I  K
E  W  K  N  V  W  I  S  L  U  Q  Z  G  Y  R
O  R  R  I  S  F  E  V  U  B  L  O  P  M  P
B  P  U  O  M  T  F  X  T  O  Z  S  O  H  Z
E  W  P  S  A  S  L  I  N  G  S  X  F  U  C
X  I  D  E  A  D  P  J  A  H  E  Q  I  D  R
F  P  R  N  D  E  W  U  H  V  R  N  L  C  Y
G  C  P  M  A  L  R  H  C  Y  L  O  I  Q  Z
Q  N  J  M  A  S  B  T  R  O  G  F  E  E  V
U  E  I  K  A  W  U  C  E  D  S  N  M  S  B
M  Z  H  R  K  P  O  H  M  X  H  Z  D  H  I
```

BRAIN	JEWELS	TREASURE
COINS	LAMP	WISH
CREATE	MAP	IDEA
GENIE	MERCHANT	RING

Vocabulary Match

Draw a line from the picture to the matching word.

   listen

                    don't listen

                    negative

   positive

   focus

   job

Aladdin's Treasure

The market was busy with people.

If only I were rich, I'd become a great merchant, thought Aladdin. *Oh well!* He looked at his tattered clothes and sighed.

Aladdin's Treasure

Color the top to make it look tattered. *Tattered* means dirty, ragged, and torn.

Aladdin's Treasure

"It's a great morning for doing tricks," said Aladdin with a grin. It was fun rolling oranges into the apple bin. He enjoyed grabbing cloth from a stand and draping it over unsuspecting customers. His favorite trick was splashing dirty water from mud puddles onto passing shoppers. However, today was different.

Aladdin's Treasure

Write a number next to each picture to show the order he did the tricks.

Favorite Trick

Try this trick:

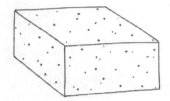

Take a 2" X 11" X 14" piece of foam and spread your favorite frosting on it.

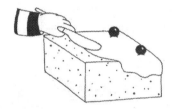

Decorate it with sprinkles or candy or make a flower and words with decorative frosting.

Who are you going to give the trick cake to? _____

Be ready for a laugh when the person tries to cut the cake.

Favorite Trick

Draw and write about your favorite trick.

Aladdin's Treasure

Carefully, he pulled the sword from his sash and held it out to the merchant. "My mom needs to sell this sword."

"Don't bother me, boy," the merchant shouted, waving Aladdin away in order to avoid his usual trouble.

Aladdin's smile faded into a frown. "I won't do that when I'm a merchant," he muttered.

Face the Feelings

How did Aladdin feel? Draw Aladdin's face showing how he felt.

What's the Feeling?

How does each child feel? Draw a line from Aladdin to his feeling word.

happy

sad

sleepy

How did Aladdin Feel?

When the merchant said, "Don't bother me, boy," how did Aladdin feel? Color the letters in the word *joy* in the puzzle below, and the remaining letters will reveal the answer.

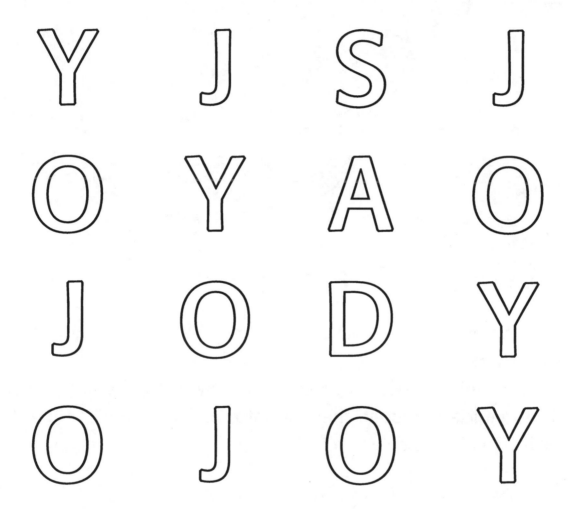

Aladdin's Treasure

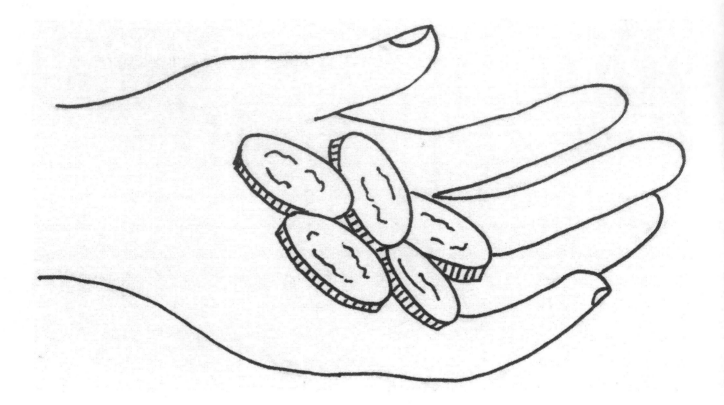

"That is a fine sword you have," said a magician. "I will give you five pieces of gold for it."

Aladdin held the sword tighter. "It was my dad's," he said softly.

The magician dropped the gold into Aladdin's hand. "Keep the sword. Instead, you do a task for me."

Aladdin's Treasure

Aladdin thought the sword was important. It was an object he treasured. He treasured it because it was his dad's. What else do you think Aladdin would treasure? Color the pictures.

My Treasures

What do you treasure?

Is there a special object?

Is there a person or animal that is important to you?

Is there an activity that makes you feel important, such as a hug?

Draw what you *treasure* next to and inside the chest.

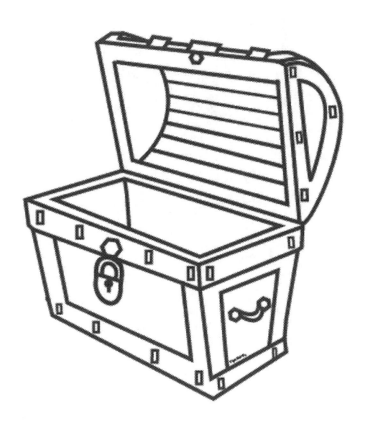

Different Treasure

Color the pictures in each row that are the same. Put an X on those that are different.

  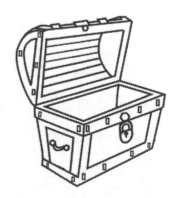

Aladdin's Treasure

"There will be enough gold to build a castle. Meet me at sunset in the garden marked on this map," the magician said.

What's in the Garden?

	A	B	C	D	E
6			🗺		
5					
4		🔥			
3					
2				🐰	
1	🐸				

Where is the bunny? <u>2D</u>
Where is the magician's map? _____
Where is the frog? _____
Where is the fire? _____

Aladdin's Treasure

At sunset, in the garden, Aladdin saw the magician leaning over a fire.

"I have a very special task for you, Aladdin." The magician threw a powder into the fire.

The Magician's Surprise

What is the surprise the magician has for Aladdin? Use the secret code below to learn the secret surprise.

___   ___   ___   ___   ___   ___

___   ___   ___   ___

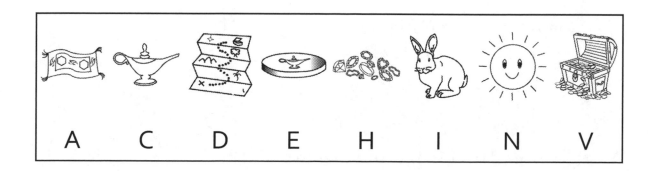

| A | C | D | E | H | I | N | V |

23

Do You Believe in Magic?

Color the happy face yes or the sad face no.

Is it magic when ...:

It is raining.

Someone gives you money.

You win at the raffle.

Your plant grows a strawberry.

You are invited to your favorite theme park.

Magic Dust

Sprinkle magic dust to create something magical. Draw and color your magical creation in the box below.

Aladdin's Treasure

The ground shook, and dirt fell away, showing a stone beneath. Aladdin backed away.

"Do not be afraid. You'll find silver, gold, and jewels beneath this stone."

The magician lifted the stone, and steps magically appeared.

Poof. It's Magic

Follow the dots to find something magical on Aladdin's hand.

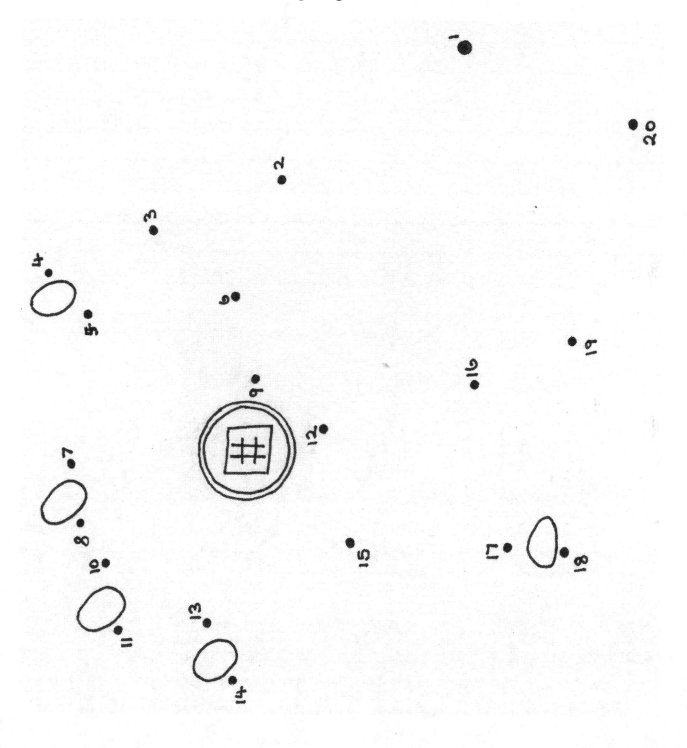

Aladdin's Treasure

At the bottom of the steps, Aladdin saw mounds of silver, gold, coins, and jewels.

Large chests were piled high with riches. "The treasure!" He grabbed handfuls of treasure and kept the lamp nestled under his arm.

Count the Treasure

Find the hidden treasure. Count and write the number of each object.

lamps _____ coins _____ treasure _____

chests_____ jewels _____ rings_____

29

The Magic

All of us create magical events, like when you hit a home run during a baseball game or get first prize at the spelling contest.

Who is creating a magical event in the story? Color the letters in the word **whoosh** in the puzzle below, and the remaining letters will reveal the answer.

A W S O

H L A O

D H D W

O S I N

Color by Numbers

Color each number, in the picture, the color listed below.

1 – gold   2 – brown   3 – blue   4 – red   5 – green   6- orange

Aladdin's Treasure

Aladdin struggled to balance it all as he climbed the stairs.
"Hand me the lamp," the magician ordered.
Clang! The lamp slipped from his hands and fell to the bottom of
the cave. Angrily, the magician threw the magic powder on the fire.

Surprise

What is the magic powder going to create?

Will it create a dog?

Will it create toys?

Draw a picture of what the magic powder will create.

Aladdin's Treasure

Aladdin fell to the stone floor, engulfed in darkness. "Where are the stairs?" he cried.

His fingers reached for the missing stairs, but he only found sand. Aladdin dug frantically.

Who Do You Listen To?

Aladdin listened to the magician who tricked him. Color the pictures that show who you listen to.

Bully

Teacher

Friend

Stranger

Family

Contest winner

What Do You Listen To?

What do you listen to? Decode the message by matching the letters to the numbers.

L ___st___n t___

3	2		4

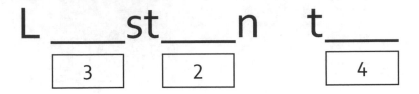

p___ ___ pl___

2	4	2

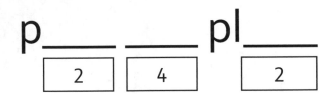

wh___   s___ ___   k___nd,

| 4 | | 1 | 6 | | 3 |

l___v___ng   w___rds.

| 4 | 3 | | 4 |

1= a   2= e   3= i   4=o   5=u   6=y

Negative Words

Throw away the words you  don't listen to.

Draw a line from the negative words to the basket of trash. Color the positive words.

You are dumb.

You are lucky.

You don't try.

You are pretty.

You are ugly.

You are terrific.

You are kind.

You are lazy.

You try hard.

You can do it.

Positive Word Search

You want to listen to these words. Can you find them hiding in the puzzle below? Look across and down.

T	S	R	R	K	Y	T	C
A	E	R	E	P	Y	H	E
E	S	R	P	N	A	H	W
R	K	A	R	M	N	I	R
G	H	J	P	I	H	I	Y
G	J	I	Z	W	F	V	W
A	O	G	N	P	X	I	K
N	G	N	I	V	O	L	C

CHAMPION   GREAT   HAPPY

LOVING   TERRIFIC   WINNER

38

You're a Star

Cut out the positive star and wear it throughout the day. One star is for you to complete.

Aladdin's Treasure

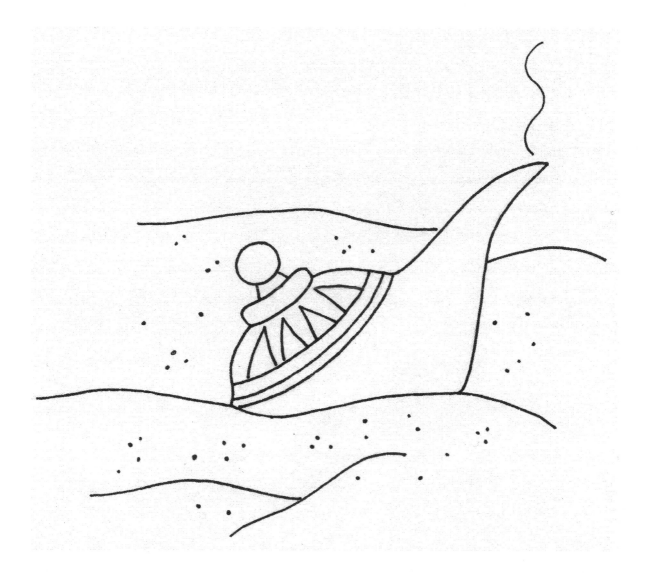

Something hard rolled out of the mound of dirt. The lamp! *Why is it so important?* He tucked it into his sash and plopped down on the stone floor of the cave.

Don't Eat Genie

1. You will need a team of two to four players.
2. Cut out the cards on the next page. Then place a piece of candy on each picture of the genie.
3. The first player picks a card. If the player gets the answer to the question correct, he or she gets to eat a piece of candy.
4. When the answer is incorrect, the turn is over.
5. Then the next person picks a card.
6. The person's turn is over when he or she picks a "Don't eat Genie!" card.
7. The next player picks a card, and the game continues until all the candy is eaten.

Don't Eat Genie Cards

Is this someone you want to listen to? You are terrific!	Is this someone you want to listen to? You are brave!	Is this someone you want to listen to? You are smart!
Is this someone you want to listen to? I love you!	Is this someone you want to listen to? You are a champion!	Is this someone you want to listen to? You have what it takes!
Is this someone you want to listen to? You are fabulous!	Is this someone you want to listen to? You can't do that!	Is this someone you want to listen to? You're not smart enough!
Is this someone you want to listen to? You can do it!	Is this someone you want to listen to? It's too hard!	Is this someone you want to listen to? I'm grateful.
Is this someone you want to listen to? I like you!	Is this someone you want to listen to? They don't like you!	Don't eat Genie!
Is this someone you want to listen to? You are lucky!	Is this someone you want to listen to? You're not good enough!	Don't eat Genie!
Is this someone you want to listen to? You are a winner!	Is this someone you want to listen to? You're dumb!	Don't eat Genie!
Is this someone you want to listen to? If it is to be it's up to me!	Is this someone you want to listen to? All your dreams are coming true.	Don't eat Genie!
Is this someone you want to listen to? You are my friend!	Is this someone you want to listen to? Who do you think you are?	Don't eat Genie!

Don't Eat Genie!

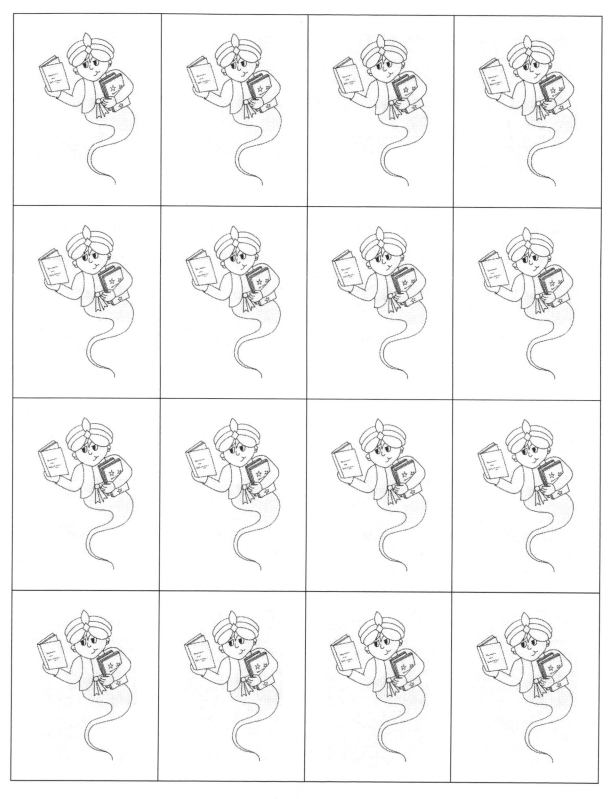

Aladdin's Treasure

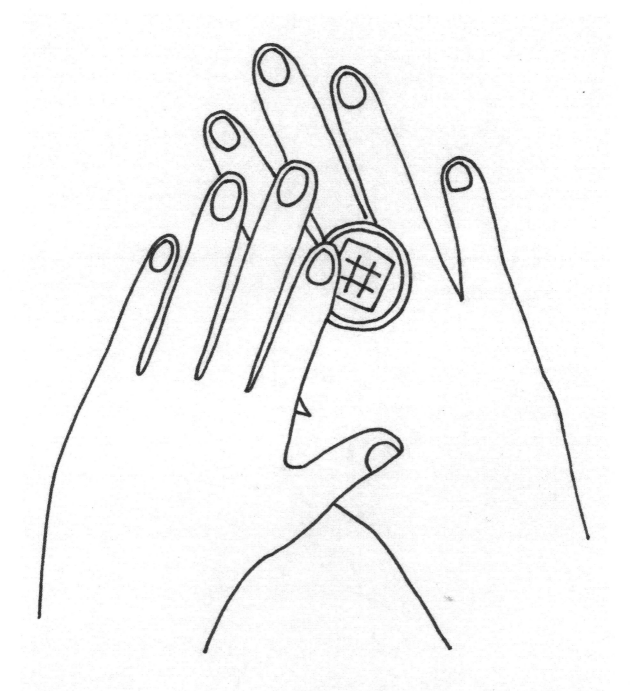

I wish I were home, Aladdin thought and rubbed his hands together.

Feels Like Magic

Feels like magic when you deep down really WISH for something and it comes true. This child has many wishes. Draw two wishes in the bubbles.

Wishes Game

How many of your wishes are coming true? The person with the most wishes at the end of the game is the winner. It is played like a game of Goldfish.

1. The game is played with two people. Each person is given six random picture cards to start the game. The remaining cards are placed in the middle of the circle.
2. Player # 1 is asked, "What is your wish?"
3. He or she will ask the other person a wish listed on one of the cards. The player may say, "I wish for a ball."
4. If the person has the wish, he or she takes the matching picture card and has a pair. The player continues to ask the other game participant until player #2 doesn't have the desired card.
5. If the person doesn't have a wish, he or she may pick a card from the middle.
6. Player #2 will go next. The player may say, "I wish for a dog."

The game is over when all the cards are in matches and the stack in the middle of the circle is gone.

7. The winner is the person with the most pairs.

Wishes Game

Cut the cards apart.

I wish for a	I wish for a	I wish for a
Teddy bear	Teddy bear	puppy
I wish for a	I wish for a	I wish for a
ball	ball	puppy
I wish for	I wish for	I wish for a
Gold coins	Gold coins	bike

Wishes Game

Cut the cards apart.

I wish for a	I wish for a	I wish for a
backpack	backpack	bike
I wish for a	I wish for	I wish for a
treasure	treasure	rabbit
I wish for a	I wish for a	I wish for a
puzzle	puzzle	rabbit

Wishes Game

Cut the cards apart.

Make two cards of your own. Copy off two or more blank cards, write in your wishes, and then draw pictures of them.

Aladdin's Treasure

Poof! A puff of smoke flashed from the ring. A tiny genie emerged and glowed like a lightbulb. "Your wish is my command," she said with a bow.

"Please. I want to go home," Aladdin cried.

Poof! Aladdin held a small toy house in his hands.

Hidden Picture

Aladdin's job was to find the lamp. What else did he find underwater?

Ring genie   treasure   map   lamp   gold coins

The Genie's Job

The genie's job is to grant your wishes.
Count how many wishes each kid got.

| 1 | 2 | 3 | 4 | 5 |

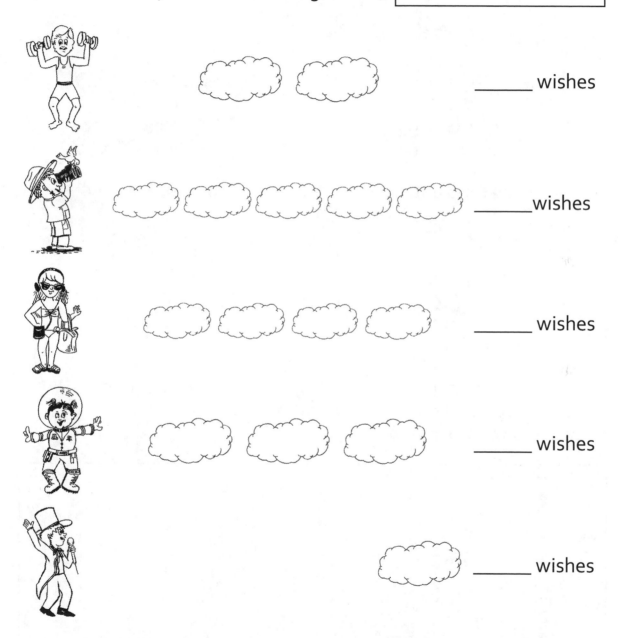

_____ wishes

_____wishes

_____ wishes

_____ wishes

_____ wishes

Do some of these kids have more than three wishes?   yes   no

Your Job

The genie's job is to grant your wishes. What are your jobs at home?
Color the pictures of your jobs.

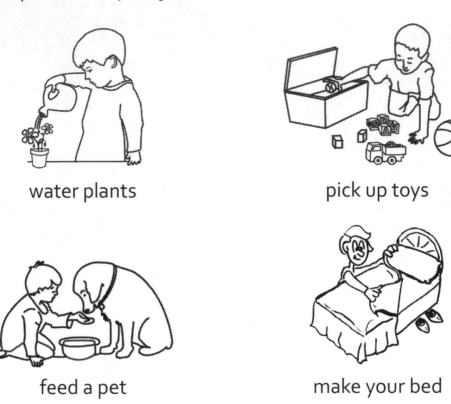

water plants

pick up toys

feed a pet

make your bed

Draw a job you do at home.

Aladdin's Treasure

"Oops! Focus!" The ring genie closed her eyes and pointed to her head. "I can see a picture of your home in my mind," she said with a giggle.

Focus

Do you need to focus to complete your job? Color the **happy** face yes or the **sad** face no. Do you focus when you

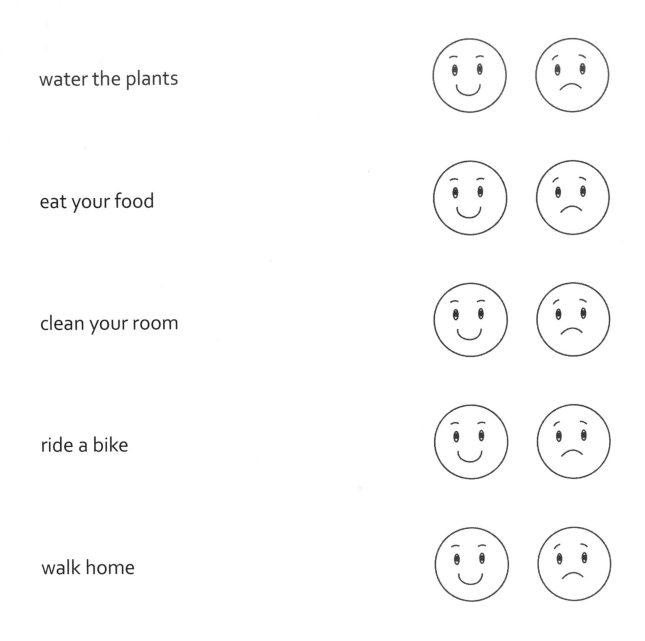

water the plants

eat your food

clean your room

ride a bike

walk home

You need to *focus* on some activities—and some activities you don't need to *focus* on.

Aladdin's Treasure

Poof! Aladdin was safely in his home.

His mom was sobbing at the table.

"Mom, I'm back," Aladdin said and lifted her with a hug. "I didn't get you the money." He grabbed the lamp from his sash. "Let's sell this instead. Please." He rubbed the lamp with his top.

Whoosh! A large genie appeared.

Genie

Color the genie of the lamp

What is a Genie?

Circle the answer to each question.

A genie is a boy or a girl. I am a _____.   boy   girl

A genie can be tall or small. I am _____.   tall   small

A genie can have long or short hair. I have _____ hair.   long   short

A genie can have brown, green, or blue eyes. I have _____ eyes.
brown   green   blue

A genie can have a big smile or a little smile. I have a _____ smile.
big   little

Where does the genie live? _____   ring   lamp   bottle

Genies are also magical. They make wishes come true. So do you.

What Do Genies Look Like?

Draw a genie. Does the genie look like you?

Aladdin's Treasure

The lamp genie was peering into a book and said, "There!" He slammed the book shut. "I love this book! I've read it more than a million times."

"Your wish is my command," the lamp genie said with a bow.

Genie's Home

Aladdin's genies lived in a ring and a lamp.

You also have a genie.

Where do you think it lives?

_____

Solve the code to find out your genie's home.

1. How many arms? _____2_____

2. How many fingers? _____

3. How many noses? _____

4. How many toes? _____

Solve the code. Finish the sentence by writing the answer to the questions on the lines below. The first one is done for you.

The genie is in your _2_ ____ _____ _____
                               1   2   3   4

Match the number with a letter below. Write it on the line.

d	a	h	m	s	v	l	o	c	t	e
0	1	2	3	4	5	6	7	8	9	10

____ ____ ____ ____

Dot-to-Dot Genie

Your genie lives in you. Follow the dots to find out where.

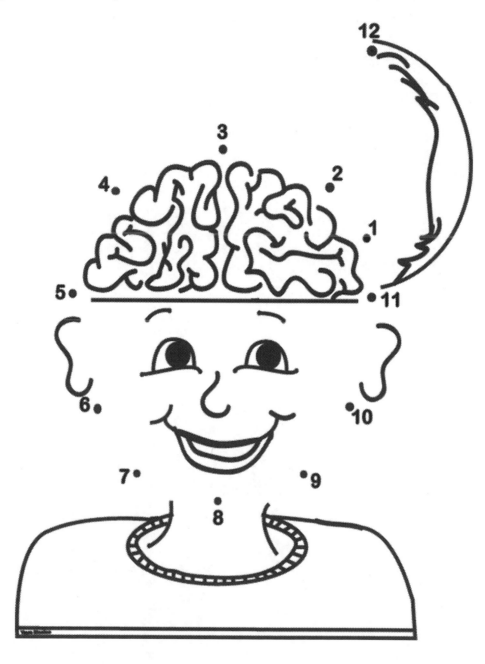

Name Your Genie

What name would you like to give your genie? _____

Since your genie is you, what does he or she like to do? _____

Draw a picture of your genie doing his or her favorite activity.

Aladdin's Treasure

"I want it the way it was before Dad died," Aladdin blurted out.

"I can't do that." The lamp genie laughed. "Genies have three rules. I can't turn back time. I can't change another person. I can't harm anyone. Other than that, you can have as many wishes as you would like."

My Wishes

How many wishes would you like? _____
Draw two of your wishes.

Aladdin's Treasure

"A feast!" Aladdin's mom shouted.

"Yes, a feast," said Aladdin.

Whoosh! A large table appeared. It was covered with all sorts of tasty food that was piled high on silver and gold dishes.

Your Magical Brain

Open the door to your brain—and then step on in.

Your brain is working—day and night.

It runs your heart—whether you are awake or asleep.

Germ-fighting cells are sent whenever you are sick.

Put your hand on your chest. You are breathing right now.

The brain's job is never done. There is more for the brain to do.

Feeling happy, mad, sleepy, or blue? Your brain creates emotions too.

When you jump for joy, the brain is excited too.

Love the taste of ice cream? It's your brain that makes the choice to like it or not like it.

Need to write your name? Your brain helps you form the letters.

Reading a book slow or fast? You're receiving messages to move your eyes from left to right.

Best of all, your brain creates like a magical genie—just wait.

Your Brain Creates

To create means to make, produce, or invent something. Your brain helps you create things. Color the pictures of the things you create. Put an X on things you don't create.

block house

picture

sun

top

Draw a picture of something you can create.

Aladdin's Treasure

Aladdin's mom said, "We can sell these dishes at the market.

A Magical Day

Solve the clues to complete the message.

1. The story is about _____'s treasure.

2.

3. The word rhymes with *flame.* The first letter is the same as in *cat.*

4. What word is the opposite of *false*?

Complete the message.

_____'s _____

1

2

_____ _____

3

4

Aladdin's Treasure

From that day forward, Aladdin did not play tricks at the market. He became a successful merchant, selling many more silver and gold dishes.

Aladdin, his mom, and the genies also enjoyed a wonderful feast every night.

Your magical treasure is always found within **YOU.**

Adapted from an Arabian folktale "Aladdin and the Wonderful Lamp" from *A Thousand and One Arabian Nights.*

Printed in the United States
By Bookmasters